Know Your Scales
and Arpeggios

(With Chords and Cadences)

by

Ada Richter

FOREWORD

This book is arranged so that it may be used by the young beginner as well as the inter-mediate and more advanced student.

In order to develop various phases of piano technique, scales and arpeggios should be played in many different ways. Variations for rhythmic, velocity, volume and finger control are therefor included. (Pages 32 to 40.) It is, of course, unnecessary to play all of these variants in every key; two or three major and minor keys will be sufficient.

Scales and arpeggios must be fingered so that it is always possible to continue to the next octave. At (a) below, the pianist is "stuck" and cannot go on to the next octave. The circled finger numbers should not be used. The fingering at (b) is correct and is used in similar cases in this book.

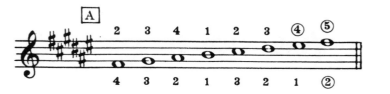 

A useful exercise for the passing under of the thumb is to play all scales that begin on a black key with the fingering used for the C major scale.

Ada Richter

CONTENTS

C MAJOR

C Major Scale
(one octave)

Key chord
or Tonic

C Major Arpeggio
(one octave)

C Major Scale (two octaves)

C Major Arpeggio
(two octaves)

Chords and Inversions on Degrees I, IV and V of the C Major Scale.
Play the Left Hand one octave lower.

I (Tonic)   IV (Subdominant)   V (Dominant)   V₇ (Dominant 7th)

Cadences in C Major.
Authentic: Authentic: Plagal: Mixed: Mixed:

V   I   V₇   I   IV   I   IV   I   V   I   IV   I   V₇   I

21889-38

G MAJOR

G Major Scale

Key chord or Tonic

G Major Arpeggio

G Major Scale (two octaves)

G Major Arpeggio (two octaves)

Chords and Inversions on Degrees I, IV, and V of the G Major Scale.
Play the Left Hand one octave lower.

I (Tonic)   IV (Subdominant)   V (Dominant)   V₇ (Dominant 7th)

Cadences in G Major.
Authentic: Authentic: Plagal: Mixed: Mixed:

V I   V₇ I   IV I   IV I V I   IV I V₇ I

D MAJOR

D Major Scale

Key chord or Tonic

D Major Arpeggio

D Major Scale (two octaves)

D Major Arpeggio (two octaves)

Chords and Inversions on Degrees I, IV and V of the D Major Scale.
Play the Left Hand one octave lower.

I (Tonic) IV (Subdominant) V (Dominant) V₇ (Dominant 7th)

Cadences in D Major.
Authentic: Authentic: Plagal: Mixed: Mixed:

V I V₇ I IV I IV I V I IV I V₇ I

A MAJOR

A Major Scale

Key chord or Tonic

A Major Arpeggio

A Major Scale (two octaves)

A Major Arpeggio (two octaves)

Chords and Inversions on Degrees I, IV and V of the A Major Scale.
Play the Left Hand one octave lower.

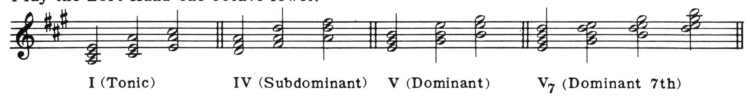

I (Tonic) IV (Subdominant) V (Dominant) V₇ (Dominant 7th)

Cadences in A Major

Authentic: Authentic: Plagal: Mixed: Mixed:

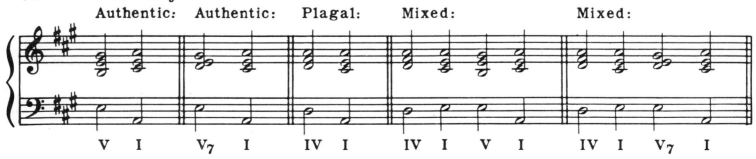

V I V₇ I IV I IV I V I IV I V₇ I

E MAJOR

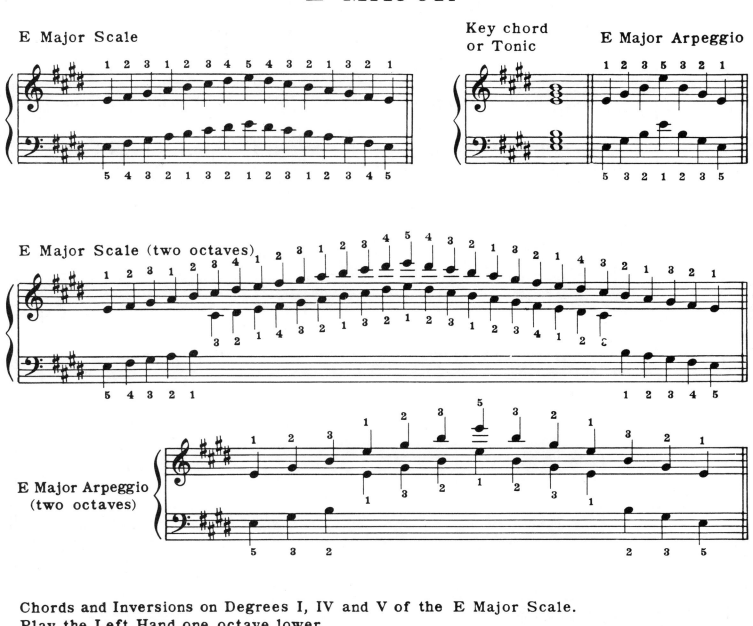

E Major Scale

Key chord or Tonic

E Major Arpeggio

E Major Scale (two octaves)

E Major Arpeggio (two octaves)

Chords and Inversions on Degrees I, IV and V of the E Major Scale.
Play the Left Hand one octave lower.

I (Tonic)   IV (Subdominant)   V (Dominant)   V₇ (Dominant 7th)

Cadences in E Major

Authentic: Authentic: Plagal: Mixed: Mixed:

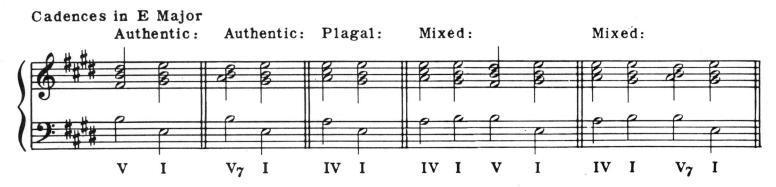

V   I   V₇   I   IV   I   IV   I   V   I   IV   I   V₇   I

B MAJOR

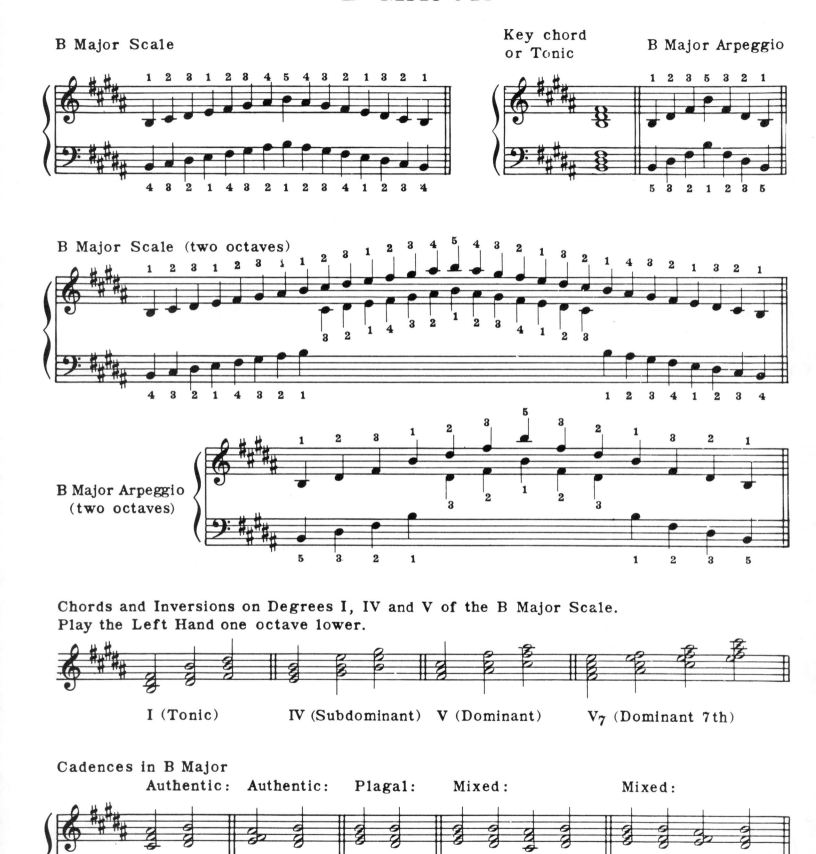

B Major Scale

Key chord or Tonic

B Major Arpeggio

B Major Scale (two octaves)

B Major Arpeggio (two octaves)

Chords and Inversions on Degrees I, IV and V of the B Major Scale.
Play the Left Hand one octave lower.

I (Tonic)   IV (Subdominant)   V (Dominant) V_7 (Dominant 7th)

Cadences in B Major

Authentic: Authentic: Plagal: Mixed: Mixed:

V   I V_7 I   IV   I   IV   I   V   I   IV   I V_7 I

F♯ MAJOR

F♯ Major Scale

Key chord or Tonic

F♯ Major Arpeggio

F♯ Major Scale (two octaves)

F♯ Major Arpeggio (two octaves)

Chords and Inversions on Degrees I, IV and V of the F♯ Major Scale.
Play the Left Hand one octave lower.

I (Tonic) IV (Subdominant) V (Dominant) V (Dominant 7th)

Cadences in F♯ Major

Authentic: Authentic: Plagal: Mixed: Mixed:

V I V₇ I IV I IV I V I IV I V₇ I

C♯ MAJOR

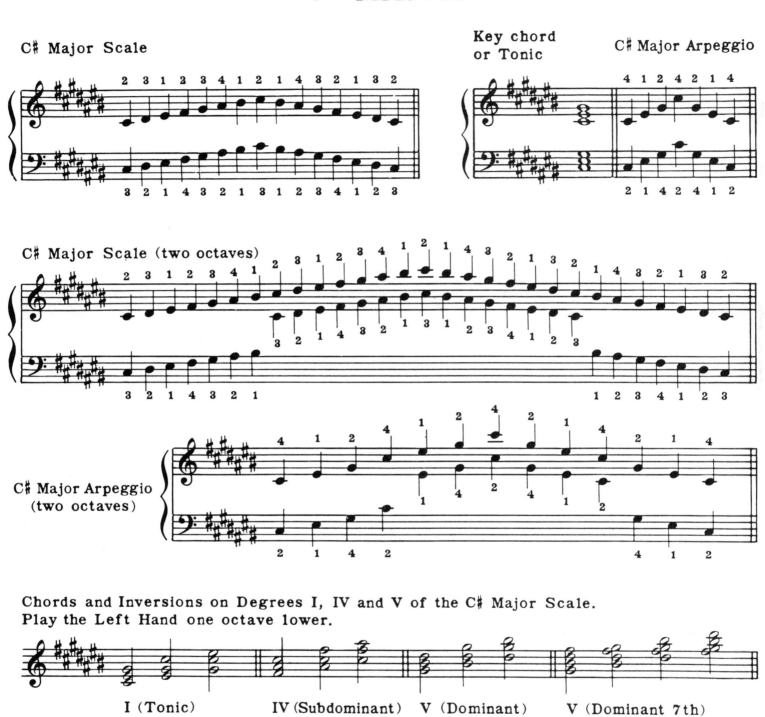

C♯ Major Scale

Key chord or Tonic

C♯ Major Arpeggio

C♯ Major Scale (two octaves)

C♯ Major Arpeggio (two octaves)

Chords and Inversions on Degrees I, IV and V of the C♯ Major Scale.
Play the Left Hand one octave lower.

I (Tonic)   IV (Subdominant)   V (Dominant)   V (Dominant 7th)

Cadences in C♯ Major

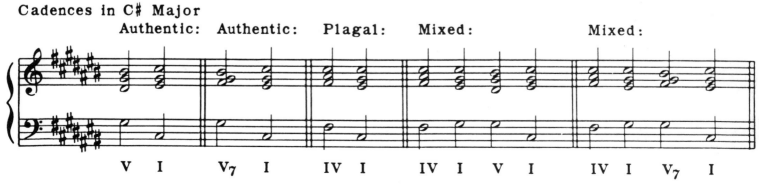

    Authentic: Authentic: Plagal: Mixed: Mixed:

V   I   V₇   I   IV   I   IV   I   V   I   IV   I   V₇   I

F MAJOR

F Major Scale

Key chord or Tonic

F Major Arpeggio

F Major Scale (two octaves)

F Major Arpeggio (two octaves)

Chords and Inversions on Degrees I, IV and V of the F Major Scale.
Play the Left Hand one octave lower.

I (Tonic)   IV (Subdominant)   V (Dominant)   V₇ (Dominant 7th)

Cadences in F Major
Authentic: Authentic: Plagal: Mixed: Mixed:

V   I   V₇ I   IV I   IV I V I   IV I V₇ I

21889-38

B♭ MAJOR

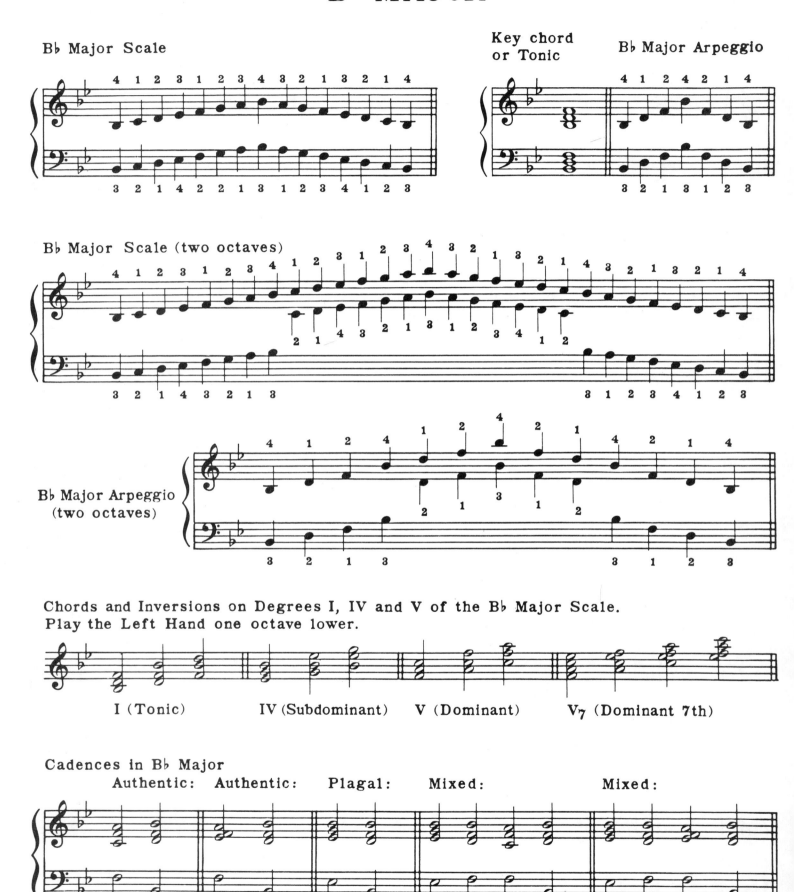

B♭ Major Scale

Key chord or Tonic

B♭ Major Arpeggio

B♭ Major Scale (two octaves)

B♭ Major Arpeggio (two octaves)

Chords and Inversions on Degrees I, IV and V of the B♭ Major Scale.
Play the Left Hand one octave lower.

I (Tonic)   IV (Subdominant)   V (Dominant)   V₇ (Dominant 7th)

Cadences in B♭ Major
Authentic: Authentic: Plagal: Mixed: Mixed:

V I   V₇ I   IV I   IV I V I   IV I V₇ I

E♭ MAJOR

E♭ Major Scale

Key chord or Tonic

E♭ Major Arpeggio

E♭ Major Scale (two octaves)

E♭ Major Arpeggio (two octaves)

Chords and Inversions on Degrees I, IV and V of the E♭ Major Scale.
Play the Left Hand one octave lower.

I (Tonic)   IV (Subdominant)   V (Dominant)   V₇ (Dominant 7th)

Cadences in E♭ Major

Authentic: Authentic: Plagal: Mixed: Mixed:

V I   V₇ I   IV I   IV I V I   IV I V₇ I

A♭ MAJOR

Ab Major Scale

Key chord or Tonic

Ab Major Arpeggio

Ab Major Scale (two octaves)

Ab Major Arpeggio (two octaves)

Chords and Inversions on Degrees I, IV and V of the Ab Major Scale.
Play the Left Hand one octave lower.

I (Tonic)   IV (Subdominant)   V (Dominant)   V₇ (Dominant 7th)

Cadences in Ab Major
    Authentic: Authentic: Plagal: Mixed: Mixed:

V I   V₇ I   IV I   IV I V I   IV I V₇ I

D♭ MAJOR

D♭ Major Scale

Key chord or Tonic

D♭ Major Arpeggio

D♭ Major Scale (two octaves)

D♭ Major Arpeggio (two octaves)

Chords and Inversions on Degrees I, IV and V of the D♭ Major Scale.
Play the Left Hand one octave lower.

I (Tonic)   IV (Subdominant)   V (Dominant)   V₇ (Dominant 7th)

Cadences in D♭ Major

Authentic: Authentic: Plagal: Mixed: Mixed:

V I   V₇ I   IV I   IV I V I   IV I V₇ I

21889-38

G♭ MAJOR

G♭ Major Scale

Key chord or Tonic

G♭ Major Arpeggio

G♭ Major Scale (two octaves)

G♭ Major Arpeggio (two octaves)

Chords and Inversions on Degrees I, IV and V of the G♭ Major Scale.
Play the Left Hand one octave lower.

I (Tonic) IV (Subdominant) V (Dominant) V₇ (Dominant 7th)

Cadences in G♭ Major

Authentic: Authentic: Plagal: Mixed: Mixed:

V I   V₇ I   IV I   IV I V I   IV I V₇ I

A MINOR

A Minor Scale-Harmonic

Key chord or Tonic

A Minor Arpeggio

A Minor Scale-Harmonic (two octaves)

A Minor Arpeggio (two octaves)

Chords and Inversions on Degrees I, IV and V of the A Minor Scale.
Play the Left Hand one octave lower.

I (Tonic)   IV (Subdominant)   V (Dominant)   V₇ (Dominant 7th)

Cadences in A Minor
Authentic: Authentic: Plagal: Mixed: Mixed:

V   I   V₇   I   IV   I   IV   I   V   I   IV   I   V₇   I

21889-38

E MINOR

E Minor Scale - Harmonic

Key chord or Tonic **E Minor Arpeggio**

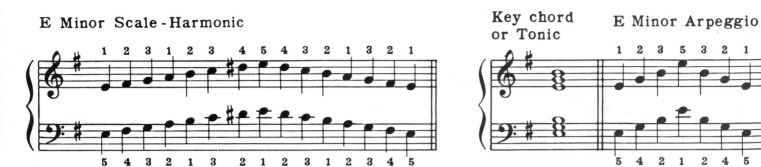

E Minor Scale - Harmonic (two octaves)

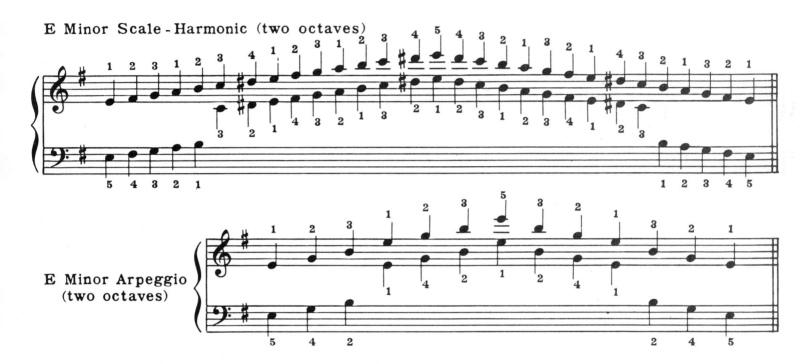

E Minor Arpeggio (two octaves)

Chords and Inversions on Degrees I, IV and V of the E Minor Scale.
Play the Left Hand one octave lower.

I (Tonic) IV (Subdominant) V (Dominant) V₇ (Dominant 7th)

Cadences in E Minor

Authentic: Authentic: Plagal: Mixed: Mixed:

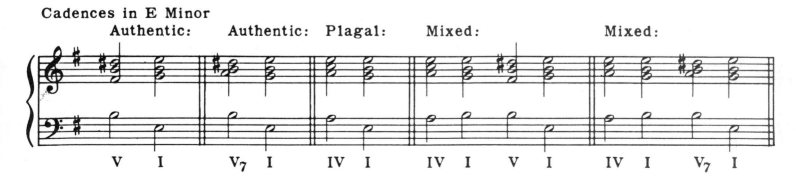

V I V₇ I IV I IV I V I IV I V₇ I

21889 - 38

B MINOR

B Minor Scale - Harmonic

Key chord or Tonic

B Minor Arpeggio

B Minor Scale - Harmonic (two octaves)

B Minor Arpeggio (two octaves)

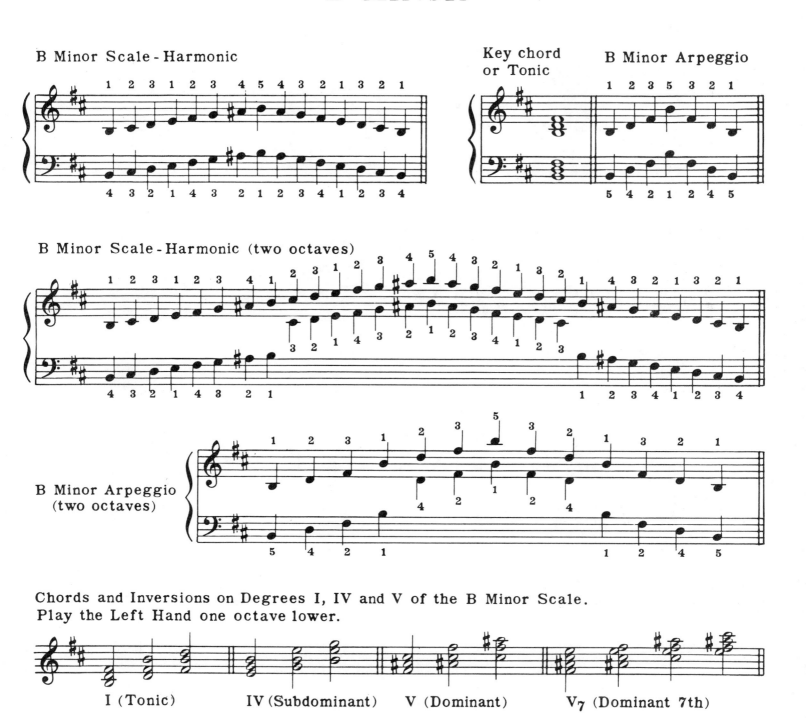

Chords and Inversions on Degrees I, IV and V of the B Minor Scale.
Play the Left Hand one octave lower.

I (Tonic)   IV (Subdominant)   V (Dominant)   V₇ (Dominant 7th)

Cadences in B Minor
Authentic: Authentic: Plagal: Mixed: Mixed:

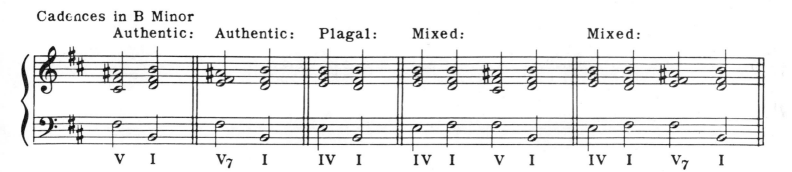

V I   V₇ I   IV I   IV I V I   IV I V₇ I

21889-38

F♯ MINOR

F♯ Minor Scale - Harmonic

Key chord or Tonic   **F♯ Minor Arpeggio**

F♯ Minor Scale - Harmonic (two octaves)

F♯ Minor Arpeggio (two octaves)

Chords and Inversions on Degrees I, IV and V of the F♯ Minor Scale.
Play the Left Hand one octave lower.

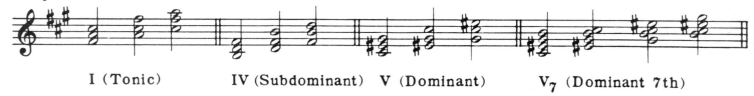

I (Tonic)   IV (Subdominant) V (Dominant)   V₇ (Dominant 7th)

Cadences in F♯ Minor
Authentic: Authentic: Plagal: Mixed: Mixed:

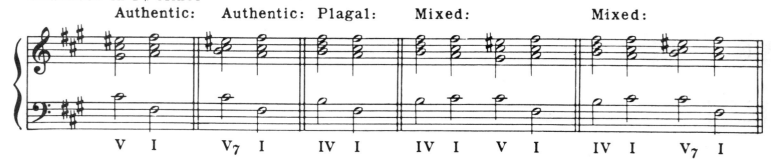

V I   V₇ I   IV I   IV I V I   IV I V₇ I

C# MINOR

C# Minor Scale - Harmonic

Key Chord or Tonic

C# Minor Arpeggio

C# Minor Scale - Harmonic (two octaves)

C# Minor Arpeggio (two octaves)

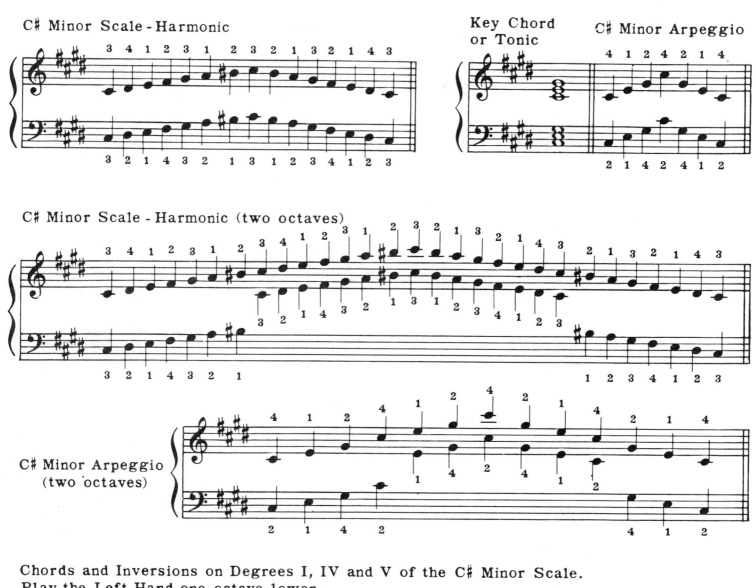

Chords and Inversions on Degrees I, IV and V of the C# Minor Scale.
Play the Left Hand one octave lower.

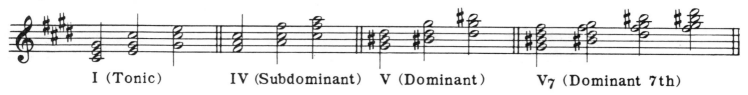

I (Tonic)   IV (Subdominant)   V (Dominant)   V₇ (Dominant 7th)

Cadences in C# Minor

Authentic: Authentic: Plagal: Mixed: Mixed:

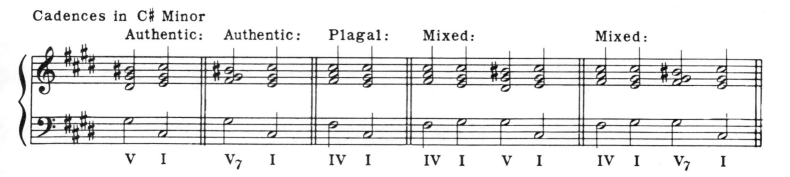

V I   V₇ I   IV I   IV I V I   IV I V₇ I

G♯ MINOR

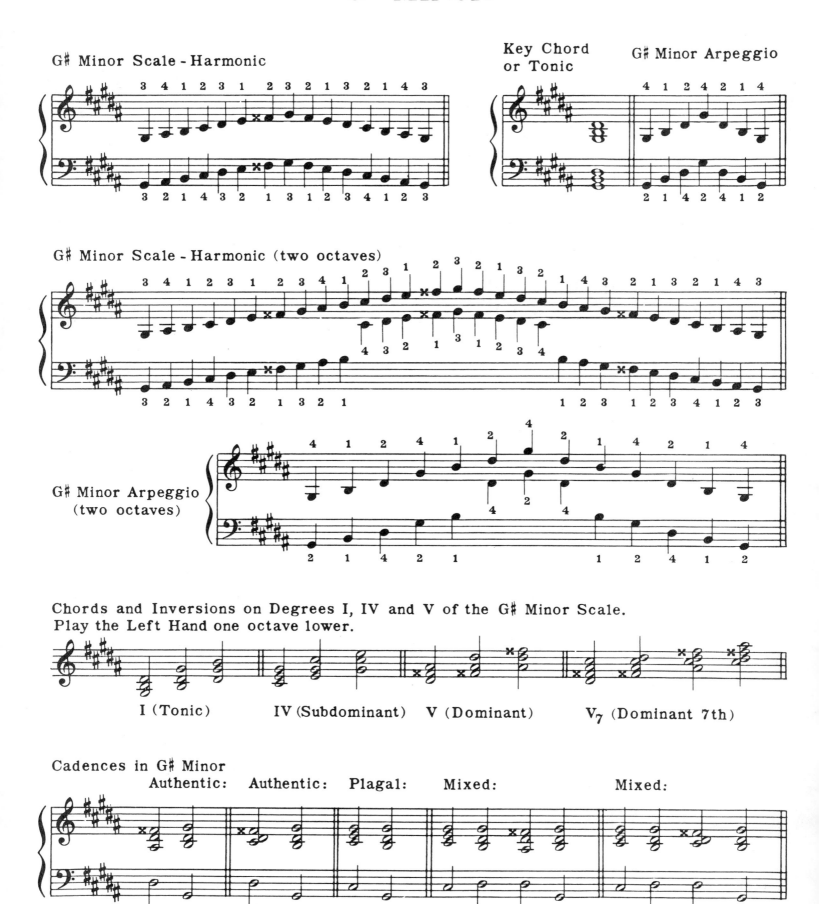

G♯ Minor Scale – Harmonic

Key Chord or Tonic

G♯ Minor Arpeggio

G♯ Minor Scale – Harmonic (two octaves)

G♯ Minor Arpeggio (two octaves)

Chords and Inversions on Degrees I, IV and V of the G♯ Minor Scale.
Play the Left Hand one octave lower.

I (Tonic)   IV (Subdominant)   V (Dominant)   V₇ (Dominant 7th)

Cadences in G♯ Minor
Authentic: Authentic: Plagal: Mixed: Mixed:

V I   V₇ I   IV I   IV I V I   IV I V₇ I

D MINOR

D Minor Scale - Harmonic

Key chord or Tonic

D Minor Arpeggio

D Minor Scale - Harmonic (two octaves)

D Minor Arpeggio (two octaves)

Chords and Inversions on Degrees I, IV and V of the D Minor Scale.
Play the Left Hand one octave lower.

I (Tonic)   IV (Subdominant)   V (Dominant)   V₇ (Dominant 7th)

Cadences in D Minor
Authentic: Authentic: Plagal: Mixed: Mixed:

V I   V₇ I   IV I   IV I V I   IV I V₇ I

21889 - 38

G MINOR

G Minor Scale - Harmonic

Key chord or Tonic

G Minor Arpeggio

G Minor Scale - Harmonic (two octaves)

G Minor Arpeggio (two octaves)

Chords and Inversions on Degrees I, IV and V of the G Minor Scale.
Play the Left Hand one octave lower.

I (Tonic)   IV (Subdominant)   V (Dominant)   V₇ (Dominant 7th)

Cadences in G Minor
Authentic: Authentic: Plagal: Mixed: Mixed:

V I   V₇ I   IV I   IV I V I   IV I V₇ I

C MINOR

C Minor Scale - Harmonic

Key chord or Tonic

C Minor Arpeggio

C Minor Scale - Harmonic (two octaves)

C Minor Arpeggio (two octaves)

Chords and Inversions on Degrees I, IV and V of the C Minor Scale.
Play the Left Hand one octave lower.

I (Tonic)   IV (Subdominant)   V (Dominant)   V₇ (Dominant 7th)

Cadences in C Minor
Authentic: Authentic: Plagal: Mixed: Mixed:

V I   V₇ I   IV I   IV I V I   IV I V₇ I

21889 - 38

F MINOR

F Minor Scale - Harmonic

Key chord or Tonic

F Minor Arpeggio

F Minor Scale - Harmonic (two octaves)

F Minor Arpeggio (two octaves)

Chords and Inversions on Degrees I, IV and V of the F Minor Scale.
Play the Left Hand one octave lower.

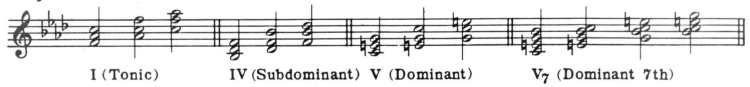

I (Tonic)   IV (Subdominant) V (Dominant)   V₇ (Dominant 7th)

Cadences in F Minor

Authentic: Authentic: Plagal: Mixed: Mixed:

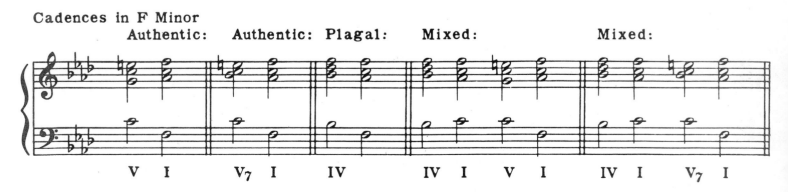

V   I   V₇   I   IV   IV   I V   I   IV   I   V₇   I

B♭ MINOR

B♭ Minor Scale - Harmonic

Key chord or Tonic

B♭ Minor Arpeggio

B♭ Minor Scale - Harmonic (two octaves)

B♭ Minor Arpeggio (two octaves)

Chords and Inversions on Degrees I, IV and V of the B♭ Minor Scale.
Play the Left Hand one octave lower.

I (Tonic)   IV (Subdominant)   V (Dominant)   V₇ (Dominant 7th)

Cadences in B♭ Minor

Authentic: Authentic: Plagal: Mixed: Mixed:

V I   V₇ I   IV I   IV I V I   IV I V₇ I

21889 - 38

E♭ MINOR

E♭ Minor Scale - Harmonic

Key chord or Tonic

E♭ Minor Arpeggio

E♭ Minor Scale - Harmonic (two octaves)

E♭ Minor Arpeggio (two octaves)

Chords and Inversions on Degrees I, IV and V of the E♭ Minor Scale.
Play the Left Hand one octave lower.

I (Tonic)   IV (Subdominant) V (Dominant)   V₇ (Dominant 7th).

Cadences in E♭ Minor

Authentic: Authentic: Plagal: Mixed: Mixed:

V I   V₇ I   IV I   IV I V I   IV I V₇ I

In the Melodic Minor Scale the 6th and 7th degrees are raised a half step ascending, lowered descending. (Descending is the Natural Minor Scale.)

This scale is a succession of half steps (or semitones). Notice that all black keys are played with the third fingers. Play the L. H. one octave lower.

In THIRDS and SIXTHS. (The same fingering as above, but the right hand begins on a note other than C.)

Major Thirds

Minor Thirds

Major Sixths

Minor Sixths

CHROMATIC SCALE IN DOUBLE MINOR THIRDS.

Preparatory Exercises. Play the scale below with two fingers - 1 and 2. Where the 2nd finger slides (2-2), slide to the side, not forward.

Now with fingers 3, 4 and 5.
R. H. ascending,　L. H. descending - the 3rd finger passes <u>over</u> the others.
R. H. descending, L. H. ascending　- the 4th and 5th pass <u>under</u> the 3rd.

Now we put them together. (Accidentals apply to one note only.)

* Slide with the 2nd finger if playing more than one octave.

(Play the scales on this page in other keys.)

C Major

C Minor (Harmonic)

C Minor (Melodic)

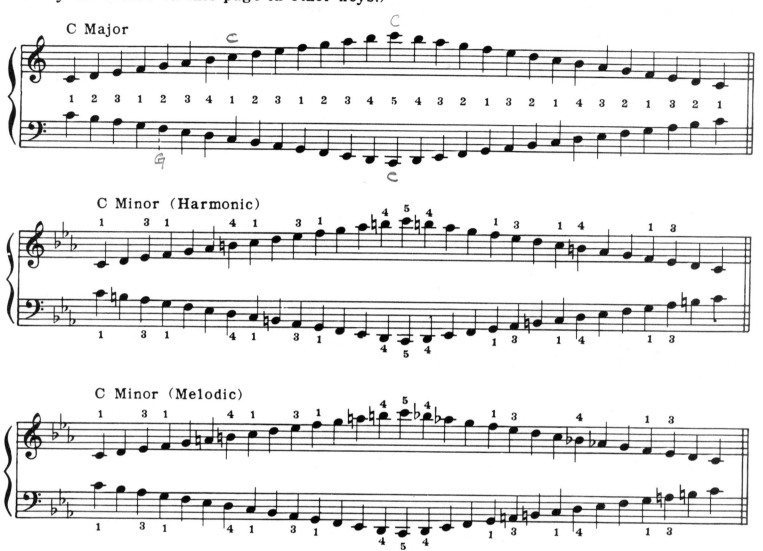

THIRDS AND TENTHS

C Major   C Minor (Harmonic)

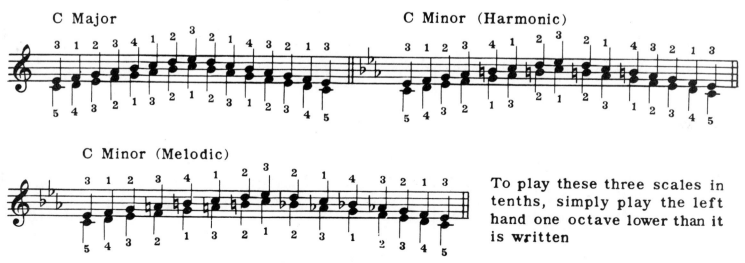

C Minor (Melodic)

To play these three scales in tenths, simply play the left hand one octave lower than it is written

SCALES for RHYTHM VELOCITY, VOLUME and FINGER CONTROL

Practice this scale without accents at first. When accents are used, be sure they are achieved by finger action alone, not wrist action. Also play it in several major and minor keys.

Four octaves in sixteenth notes (♪♪♪♪) and five octaves in sixteenth quintuplets
(♪♪♪♪♪) may be added to the above.

Canon

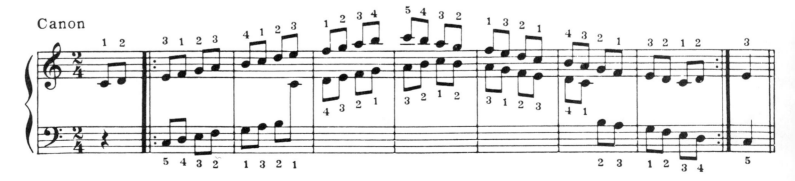

EIGHTH NOTE TRIPLETS

DOTTED EIGHTH AND SIXTEENTHS, EIGHTH NOTES, EIGHTH NOTE TRIPLETS

DOTTED EIGHTH AND SIXTEENTHS, EIGHTH NOTE TRIPLETS AND SIXTEENTH NOTES

QUARTER, EIGHTH NOTE TRIPLETS, SIXTEENTH NOTES, SIXTEENTH QUINTUPLETS

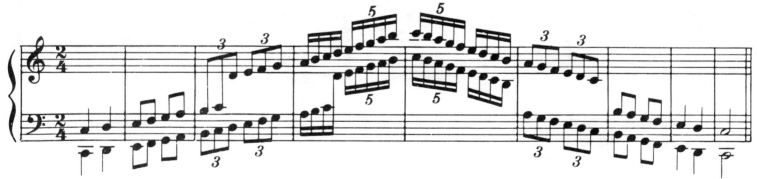

TWO AGAINST THREE. (If the parts are reversed, begin two octaves apart.)

The variations below are numbered for easy assignment by the teacher, for example: I in C minor, IV in A major, etc. They may be extended to more than two octaves; played in contrary motion, in thirds, tenths, or in various rhythmic patterns, staccato and legato.

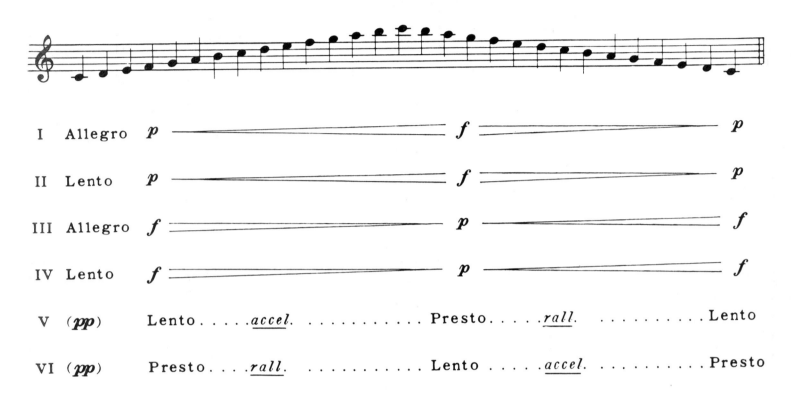

VII Accent and pause a long time on the keynotes. The grace notes are to be played as rapidly, softly and evenly as possible.

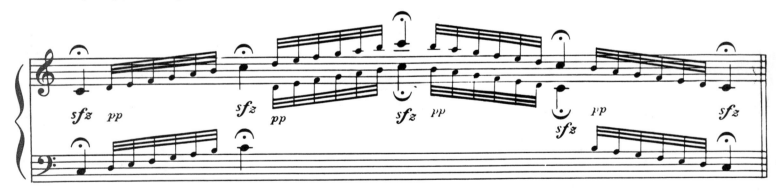

ARPEGGIOS for RHYTHM, VELOCITY, VOLUME and FINGER CONTROL

Play these arpeggios *p*, *f*, *cresc.*, ascending - *dim.*, descending, with and without accents, staccato, legato, and in several Major and Minor keys.

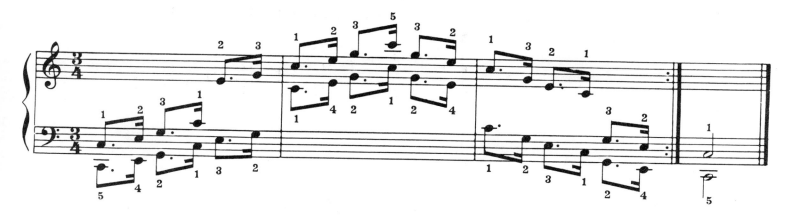

Play this one also with 8th notes in R. H., dotted 8ths and 16ths in L. H.

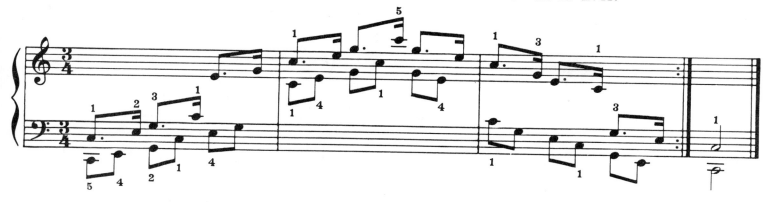

In strict time. (Quarters, eighths, eighth triplets, sixteenths.)

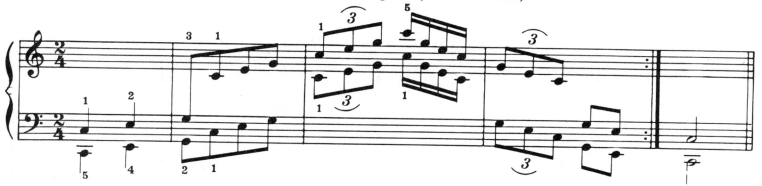

Two against three. (When playing the triplets with the L. H., begin R. H. one octave higher.)

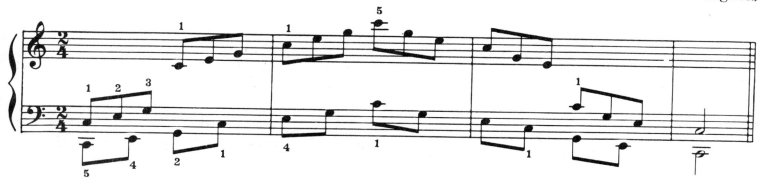

ARPEGGIOED CHORDS - THREE POSITIONS. (Notice that in each position we use fingers 1, 2 and 5; the remaining note is played by either 3 and 4. These two finger numbers are circled in the exercises below.)

C Major

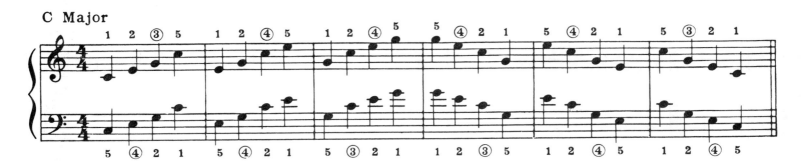

Use the C Major fingering above for these keys:

     G Maj.   F Maj.   A Min.   E Min.   D Min.

D Major

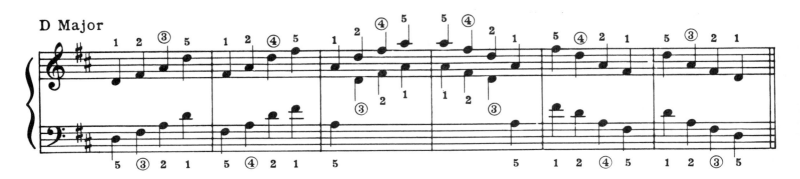

Use the D Major fingering above for these keys:

   A Maj.   E Maj.   B Maj.   F# Maj.   Bb Maj.   Eb Maj.   Ab Maj.   Db Maj.

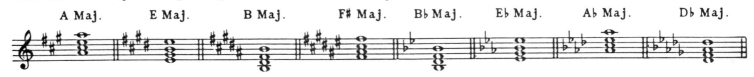

B Minor

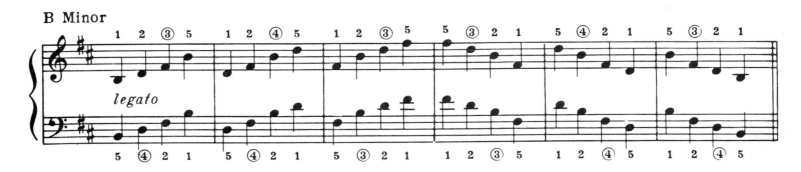

Use the B Minor fingering above for these keys:

   F# Min.   C# Min.   G# Min.   G Min.   C Min.   F Min.   Bb Min.   Eb Min.

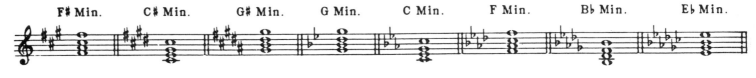

ARPEGGIOED CHORDS - DOMINANT 7th (Four Positions.)

Play these arpeggios piano, forte, *cresc.*, ascending - *dim.*, descending, etc.
Play them in several other keys. (The dominant 7th is the same in both Major and Minor.)

Although the R.H. usually uses the 4th finger in the first position in the exercise below,
the 3rd finger (in parenthesis) permits greater velocity.

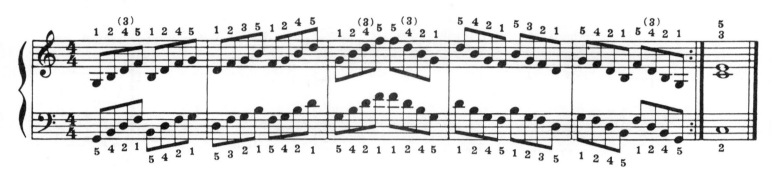

RHYTHMIC VARIATION. The fingering is the same as above.

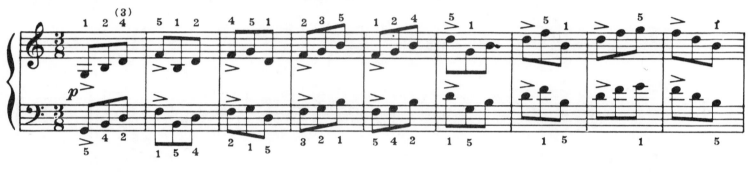

CROSSING HANDS. (The L.H. goes <u>over</u> the R.H. ascending, the R.H. goes <u>over</u>
the L.H. descending.)

(Vary these arpeggios in the same manner as suggested on the preceding pages.)

RHYTHMIC VARIATION - Dominant 7th (Cross Hands.)

(L. H. over R. H. ascending; R. H. over L. H. descending.)

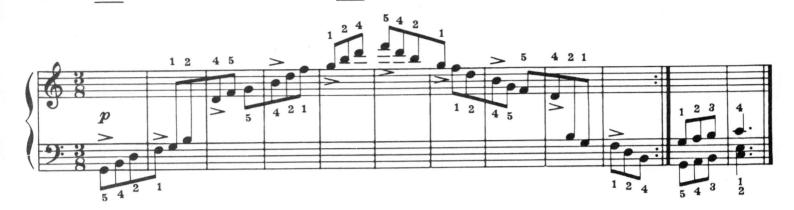

ALTERNATE HANDS - WITH ACCENTS. (The L.H. over the R.H. both ascending and descending.)

HANDS TOGETHER

WITH AND WITHOUT ACCENTS

DOMINANT SEVENTH

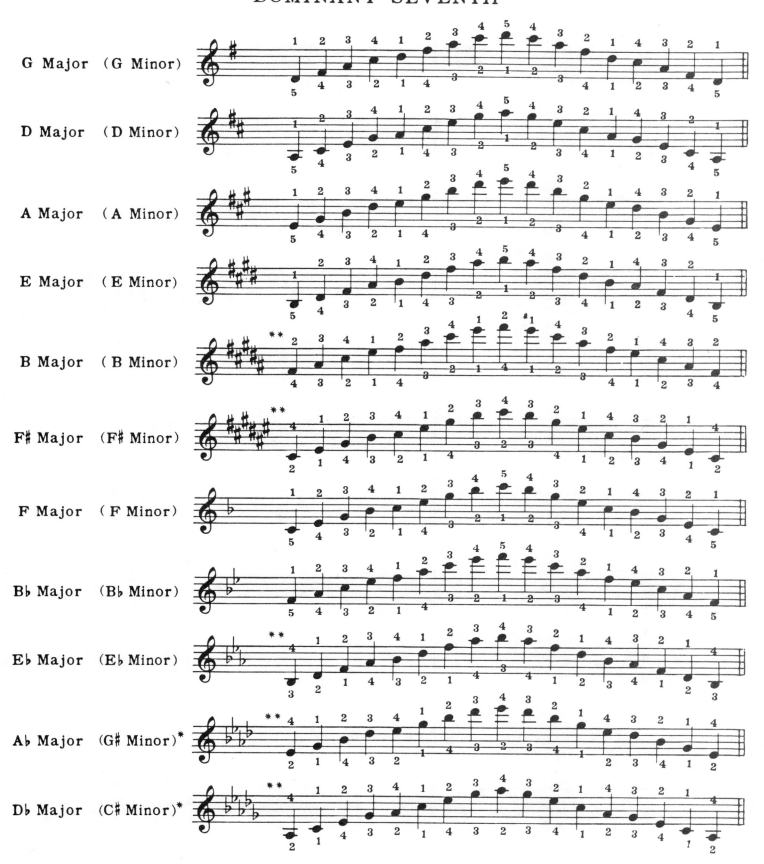

* These are the parallel minor scales mostly used. The dominant 7th chord <u>sounds</u> exactly the same in both keys.

** This fingering makes a legato execution possible. However, for finger development, these arpeggios should be practiced with the G major fingering.

THREE DIMINISHED 7th ARPEGGIOS (Postpone this page for very small hands.)

Play these arpeggios in various ways - legato, staccato, piano, forte, with and without accents; *cresc.*, ascending, *dim.*, descending etc. When playing them with accents, play them in triplets so that every finger has a note to accent: (𝅘𝅥 𝅘𝅥 𝅘𝅥 𝅘𝅥 𝅘𝅥 𝅘𝅥).

TWO VARIATIONS FOR WEAK FINGERS

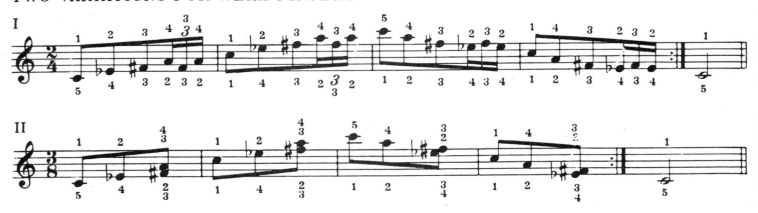